BYLAND ABBEY

NORTH YORKSHIRE

❖

Stuart A Harrison

The abbey of Byland was regarded in its heyday as one of the three great monasteries of the north, alongside Rievaulx and Fountains. But its beginnings were unpromising: it was only after forty-three years, and numerous moves from one unsuitable site to another, that the community of Byland found its permanent home. It started life across the Pennines as a monastery of the reforming order of Savigny, founded from Furness Abbey in Cumberland, and was absorbed into the larger Cistercian order in 1147.

The remains of the abbey are remarkable for the exceptionally large cloister and the scale of the church, reflecting the size of the community which once lived here. The beautiful west front, with its ruined great rose window, is an outstanding example of early Gothic architecture.

❖ CONTENTS ❖

Published by English Heritage
1 Waterhouse Square, 138-142 Holborn, London EC1N 2ST
© English Heritage 1999
First published by English Heritage 1999
This edition first published 1999, reprinted 2002, 2006, 2009
Revised reprint 2010, 2012, 2015
Photographs, unless otherwise specified, were taken by English Heritage
Photographic Unit, and remain the copyright of English Heritage

Edited by Louise Wilson
Designed by Pauline Hull. Plans by Hardlines
Printed in England by Pureprint Group Ltd
C45 01/15 05613 ISBN 978 1 85074 739 0

TOUR OF THE ABBEY

❖

THE CHURCH

*From the ticket office walk over to the
ruins of the great church and enter by
the central doorway.*

The church is the largest single building
at Byland, exceeding many contemp-
orary cathedrals in size. It was built
to a plan traditional in Cistercian
monasteries, a simple cruciform or
cross shape with the longest part laid
out from east to west and two side arms
(the north and south transepts). It is
100m (330 ft) long and 43m (140 ft)
wide across the transepts.

Cistercian churches were built
essentially to serve two communities of
monks. The choir monks, who spent a
large proportion of their time in church,
occupied the east end of the church (the
choir), while the lay brothers, who spent
much of their time in manual work
and attended fewer, simpler services,
used the western part of the nave.

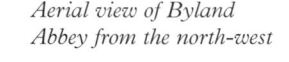

*Aerial view of Byland
Abbey from the north-west*

❖ ARCHITECTURAL IMPORTANCE ❖

The design of the church was by far the most elaborate attempted by the Cistercians at that time in England, and broke away from their previous adherence to simple, plain churches. With its galleried upper walls, brightly painted decoration, and new handling of light and space, it reached a splendour far removed from the earlier Cistercian buildings with their relatively plain walls and small windows. Its place in the development of Gothic architecture cannot be over-emphasised, as it was one of the first buildings in the north fully to break away from the Romanesque tradition. It was copied in both details and main design at nearby Old Malton Priory, and also at Tynemouth Priory.

It is very difficult to appreciate how magnificent the design of the church was, for all the great arcades and the central tower collapsed many years ago. The parts which survive are of the highest quality, both in mason-craft and design, and contrast with the plainness and rough work of the cloister buildings. The great capitals (column heads) set into the aisle walls show an infinite variety of detail, with waterleaf, crocket and volute forms. Sadly, many of these are now decaying, but during the excavation many capitals and corbels were recovered and the best of these are now displayed in the site museum. They show the quality of carving at its most excellent, and in some instances traces of painted decoration.

When first completed, the church was limewashed inside, with false masonry lines painted in red, a theme carried into the walls of the chapels which in places had painted vine scroll patterns and flowers. Some of the main columns were also decorated with vine leaf and scale pattern, and all the carved capitals were highlighted by having their details picked out in red. The plain, cup-shaped capitals were also painted in red to imitate those of carved form. In the later period, when the floors were tiled, the aisle walls were decorated with figurative paintings, including a depiction

DRAWING BY PETER URMSTON

Reconstruction of the Romanesque nave at St Augustine's Abbey, Canterbury, showing how colourful churches were at this time

West front

Dominating the ruins are the remains of the west front of the church. This was the last part of the church to be completed. It had a complex building history, the evidence for which is still apparent in places as described below.

The main feature of the design is the great rose window. Though a traditional Cistercian feature, here it seems to have been an afterthought. The blocking up of the stair turret on its south side and the triple shafts which divide the three pointed (lancet) windows internally, suggest that the

Decorated capital and corbel in the site museum

of the dead Christ on His Mother's knee on the wall of the north aisle of the nave, which has long since perished.

The windows would have been glazed with silvery glass known as grisaille, set in lively geometrical leaded patterns, while in the later period, coloured glass windows with figurative scenes were introduced. Broken fragments of these were found during excavation.

Comparative drawing of four rose windows from Cistercian abbeys in Yorkshire

Byland Abbey

Fountains Abbey

Kirkstall Abbey

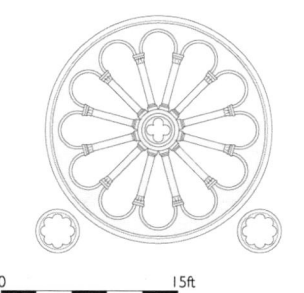

Fountains Abbey: west

0   5m   0   15ft

Reconstruction drawing of the inside of the church by Simon Hayfield

original design was for three lancet windows in the gable. Instead, the rose window was adopted.

It has recently proved possible to identify enough pieces of tracery (stonework divisions) to make an accurate reconstruction of the rose window. We know from excavation that the master mason designed the main part of its tracery upon the floor of the room above the warming house, but he also inscribed the central detail of the tracery upon the inside wall of the west front of the church, just north of the central doorway, where it is still just visible on a dull day. The Byland window resembled the rose window in the south transept of York Minster and seems to have formed the model for that design.

The three doorways in the west front of the church were originally hidden by a porch known as the galilee, now ruined to its lowest courses. The position of its roof against the front can be seen in the row of projecting corbel brackets which served as supports. Curiously, those over the southern doorway (on your right as you face the church), are set at a lower level and show that this was the first part to be finished. All the others were set higher because the central doorway was enlarged and heightened during construction. The doorway to the south aisle of the church is different from the

other doors in that it is round-headed, showing that this too was of earlier date.

Walk ahead of you down the long nave of the abbey church.

Nave

The first six bays of the nave, or main body of the church, were given over to the choir of the lay brothers (see page 17).

The columns here had square fronts to enable the lay brothers' tiered stalls to stand against them, although above the stalls they changed to columns with eight shafts (see drawing opposite). When lay brothers ceased to form part of the community, their stalls were cleared and this part of the nave became an open space used for processions. Part of the aisle space was sub-divided into extra chapels.

The next two bays of the nave formed the retrochoir, in which those monks too old or infirm to take part

The west front of the church in the nineteenth century

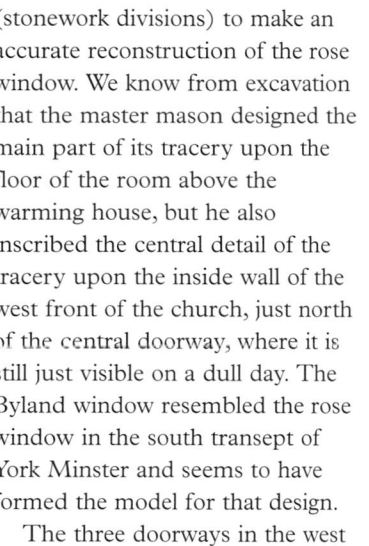

The west front today, showing the row of projecting stone brackets which once supported a porch

Below: View east down the nave

Drawing of the south transept in around 1810 by Henry Cave

The tiled floor of the presbytery and the re-erected arcading

in the services could sit and hear them. The retrochoir was enclosed on its west side by a screen called the rood, which would have carried an image of Christ upon the cross.

The three eastern bays of the nave were occupied by the monks' choir stalls, and on the north side are the remains of part of the sub-base which supported these. This is of late date and indicates that the stalls were refurbished at least once, possibly as a result of the reduction in the number of monks. The stalls were bounded on their west side by another screen known as the pulpitum.

Crossing and tower

This is the central crossing of the church, where the arms or transepts of the cross-shape meet the nave. Before the step up into the presbytery are the remains of the grave slabs of two of the abbots. Before the Dissolution of the Monasteries they held brasses.

Over the crossing there was once a tower. The Cistercians were only permitted to build towers on their churches provided that they were not too high and did not house bells.

Fallen parts of the central tower of this abbey, which were found in excavation, show that it was supported on four large pointed arches and had windows which admitted light into the crossing below. These would have been very similar to that shown by Cave's drawing in the gable of the south transept (left). Internally it would have seemed a very high tower, but externally probably only rose one stage above the steeply pitched roofs of the church. It was probably capped by a wooden spire covered, like most of the abbey buildings, with flat, red roofing tiles.

North transept

The north transept or side arm of the church (to your left) was probably built at almost the same time as the eastern arm. Both these parts of the church have columns with twelve shafts, but in the nave and south transept these are changed to eight shafts, showing an alteration in the course of building. In both north and south transepts, there are two eastern chapels and a western aisle.

East end

The five chapels in a row against the far (east) wall of the church stand on raised platforms, and were formerly

divided from each other by walls. These chapels formed an eastern aisle round the east gable wall which was supported upon three arches.

The high altar was enclosed within the ritual presbytery. This was three bays long, flanked by stone-vaulted aisles, and enclosed by decorative screen walls. Parts of this thirteenth-century arcading, which were found collapsed during excavation, have been re-erected on the north side. The table of the high altar was removed in 1820 by a former owner of the abbey, and given in 1870 to the monks of nearby Ampleforth Abbey, where it is now in use as the altar of St Benet's Chapel. Flanking the altar on the south side would have been the sedilia or seats for the priests celebrating the high mass.

South transept

The south transept collapsed in 1822, and much of our knowledge of how it originally appeared is gained from earlier drawings. We know from a drawing dating from 1801 by Thomas Atkinson (below) that the south transept gable had two rows of pointed windows in its upper wall with a stair turret up the centre. Cave's drawing, opposite, also shows some detail, particularly of the capitals – some plain and some elaborately carved.

It is in the south transept that much of the magnificent tiled floor of the church still survives. At first, the floor of the church, apart from some of the chapels, was probably of beaten earth strewn with rushes, but in the thirteenth century the whole church seems to have been repaved

Drawing by Thomas Atkinson, 1801

Above: The tiled floor of the south transept
Below: A drawing of the tiles in the south transept, made in about 1929 shortly after their discovery, by J S Richardson

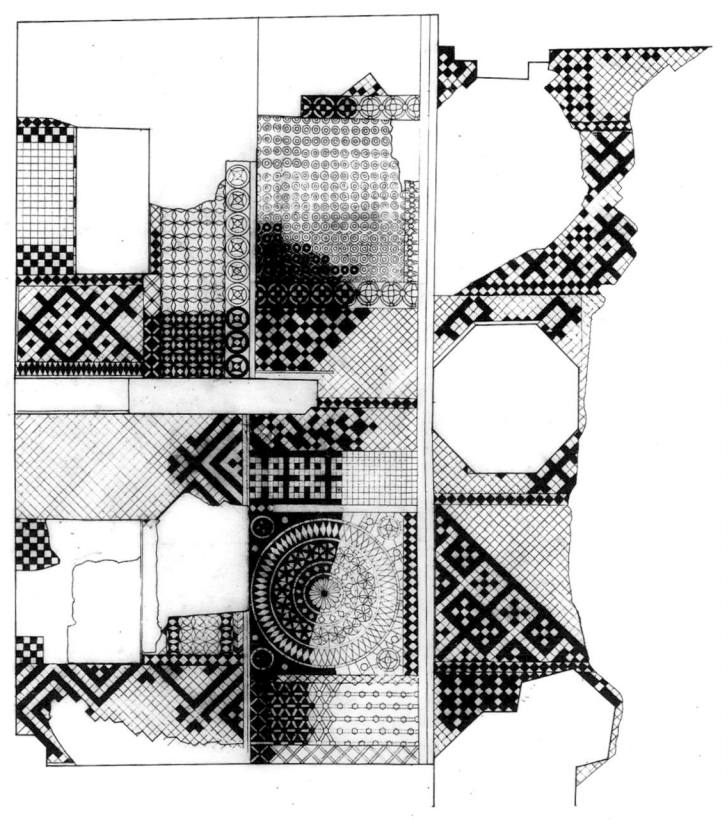

with tiled floors, with intricate geometrical patterns. Extensive areas of this paving were found intact during excavation and, although the glaze is much worn, the floors in the chapels of the south transept give a clear impression of the overall effect.

In the south wall of this transept, in an inserted arched recess, is a piscina or washing bowl with three drains. Another one lies on the dividing wall between the chapels. These piscinas were provided at all the altars in the church for cleaning the altar vessels after Mass.

The western aisle of the south transept was filled by the stairs from the monks' dormitory, used to enter the church for the night services. Only the lowest treads now remain.

The piscina in the south wall of the south transept

DOMESTIC BUILDINGS

Leave the church via the stair in the south wall of the south transept.

This leads down into a passage with a vestry to the east (your left), entered down a flight of steps from the church, and a library to the west.

Turn right into this passageway until you meet the cloister. Then turn right and left into the north alley.

NORTH CLOISTER RANGE

You are now in the cloister, which is set some feet below the level of the church. The great cloister at Byland was one of the largest in the country, 44.2m (145ft) square, reflecting the great size of the community in its heyday. It had covered alleys on all four sides, originally supported on open arcades. In the fifteenth century, as part of a general move towards greater comfort, the cloister was rebuilt with glazed windows.

The west, south and east alleys were principally passageways, but the north alley (the one you are in now) would have been subdivided by timber or stone partitions into carrels, or small private studies, in which the monks could read or copy manuscripts. In the centre of the north wall, facing the garth or central area, is a doorway of thirteenth-century date, which gave access to a small projecting, vaulted

porch. This was where the reader stood to deliver the final Collation reading of the day.

When not in church or performing manual tasks, the monks spent much of their time in the cloister, and were forbidden to leave it. It was also the place where they would periodically shave their heads, have their beards trimmed, and hang their washing out to dry.

Below: View of the great cloister from the south-west

Bottom: Reconstruction of the cloister at Cleeve Abbey by Terry Ball. The alleys at Byland would have looked very similar until the fifteenth century

A recess in the wall of the chapter house

Above: The carved lectern base. Right: Inkwell with holes for quill pens

View inside the chapter house

Retrace your steps eastwards along the north alley, and turn right so that you are in the east alley again.

EAST CLOISTER RANGE

The east side of the cloister is taken up with the quarters of the choir monks, and is subdivided following the plan common to Cistercian monasteries. The whole of the first floor formed their dormitory, from which a stair at the north end led down into the south transept of the church for the night services. At the north end of the cloister alley, a pair of recesses, now much ruined, were probably used as book cupboards.

Chapter house

South of the passage next to the transept is the chapter house, entered through a fine central doorway. Here the monks met daily to discuss Abbey business. It was called the Chapter House because a chapter from the Rule of St Benedict was read out at every meeting. The monks sat on the tiered bench seats around the walls. The abbot sat at the centre of the east wall, with obedientiaries (officials) on either side.

The floor level is several steps below that of the cloister, allowing greater height for the stone ribbed vaults of its roof. Only one column of the original four which supported the vaults now remains, together with some of the brackets set into the side walls to support the vaults. One original tomb slab survives in the floor, together with the modern cover of another grave. Originally there would have been a lot more, for this was the burial place of many abbots, and tomb slabs in the churches of Kilburn, Oswaldkirk and Brafferton were probably stolen from here. At the east end of the side walls are arched recesses which also contained tombs.

During the excavation of the chapter house in 1924, two objects of interest were found: a pottery inkwell, with holes for quill pens, probably used by the last abbot and monks to sign the deed surrendering the abbey to the king; and the stone base of the lectern used during chapter meetings. This is the only

lectern base so far found in a chapter house in England; it has now been restored. Both are on display in the recently refurbished site museum.

Parlour

Next to the chapter house is the parlour – the only room off the cloister where the monks were permitted to speak, and then only for essential communication. Benches flank the side walls, and the springers for the vaulting remain on the south wall. South of the parlour was another passage through the range, flanked on the south side by the day stairs to the dormitory, which partially intrude into it.

Reredorter

The next left turn from the east alley is a passage that leads east to the ground floor of the monks' latrine or reredorter. Following the usual plan, this had a great drain down its centre, screened by walls. Over the drain, at first floor level, would have been a row of latrines, the drain below being flushed by running water. The north wall of the reredorter was a continuation of the passage through the east range, pierced by a row of open arches which were later blocked. At the east end, a covered way, or pentice, led northward to the doorway in the south aisle wall of the church. A covered passage also formed the south side of the reredorter, but only

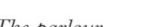

Day stairs to the dormitory

traces of this now remain. This reredorter was replaced by a new one in the early thirteenth century because of drainage problems. The new one was built at right angles to the east end of the old one and had a revised drainage system, with a similar drain screened from the basement by side walls. In later years a fireplace was inserted into the east wall to provide greater comfort.

Return to the cloister via the passage and enter the next room in the east range, south of the day stairs.

Workroom (dayroom)

Here there is a large vaulted room, used originally by the monks for manual work: it is divided by a central row of columns into seven bays. Its use for the storage of tools and as a workshop is highlighted by the fact that its east wall was supported upon a row of open arches originally closed by timber doors. It was later extended and divided into small rooms to form the

The parlour

The reredorter

The undercroft of the dormitory from the north

monks' living quarters and infirmary in the fifteenth century - a time when individual privacy was becoming more of a priority.

Infirmary site

The rooms built out to the east at this later period were probably on the site of the original infirmary. All Cistercian abbeys had large infirmary buildings for the care of monks who were sick, old or infirm, and for those monks who had been bled – regular bleeding at certain times of the year was thought to be beneficial. No trace now survives of this building at Byland, although it

BRITISH LIBRARY

Monks in the infirmary, from an illuminated manuscript

would certainly have existed.

The later years of the abbey saw a reduction in the number of monks, with a small number of monks using buildings designed for hundreds. This led to considerable changes in the way that the buildings were used. It seems most likely that the infirmary was demolished simply because it was too large and old; re-used twelfth-century material in the later ranges of buildings may represent parts of its structure.

Retrace your steps towards a smaller building just to the south-west of the east range.

Meat kitchen

Here there is a small room with a large fireplace set into each wall, which was the meat kitchen of the monastery, built in the fifteenth century. There is a large doorway on the south side, for bringing in provisions. By this later date the monks were allowed to eat meat on a regular basis, but the regulations stated that it had to be cooked in a separate kitchen and eaten in a separate refectory. No trace remains of the meat refectory, but it seems likely that part of the south end of the dormitory was converted to its use.

Abbot's lodging

To the south of the east range lie the much ruined remains of a large free-standing building, which was the abbot's lodging. Its plan follows the typical arrangement of a medieval hall, found in castles and large houses as well as monasteries. At the west end, a cross-wing formed the buttery (liquor store) and pantry. This wing joined the main hall, which is of thirteenth-century date with its main doorway in the north-west corner. Towards the east end is a hearth in the middle of the floor, and no doubt there would have been a louvre for the smoke to escape from the roof above. The hall was originally much longer, but was reduced in size by the insertion of another cross-wing of late date at the east end. This later wing has two ground-floor rooms with large windows in the north wall and

a substantial chimney stack set in the dividing wall. In front of the fireplace is a considerable area of stone paving which bordered a tiled central area.

Adjoining, to the east, is the oldest part of the range, a vaulted undercroft built around 1190 which has traces of an earlier building incorporated into its west wall. This formed the abbot's private solar or sleeping quarters, on the first floor. A now vanished building, which was traced during excavation, projected eastwards from the south-east corner of the block. The ground floor of this was a well house and the first floor may have housed the abbot's private chapel.

When the monastery was dissolved, this range of buildings was allowed to stand intact and was given over to the use of a farmer, but by the end of the eighteenth century it had fallen into ruin.

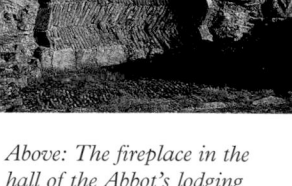

Above: The fireplace in the hall of the Abbot's lodging

Left: The vaulted undercroft of the Abbot's lodging

❖ LIFE IN THE MONASTERY ❖

The Cistercian Order placed great stress upon the strict observance of the Rule of St Benedict and the monastic vows of poverty, chastity and obedience. A Cistercian monastery like Byland was an island of devotion to God amidst an often unruly and strife-torn world. As such, it was inward-looking and sought to cut itself off from everyday life. It worked to a strict hierarchical system, all the monks owing obedience to the abbot who governed their lives as a father.

A number of officers called obedientiaries administered the daily running of the monastery and the estates, which in a large house such as Byland was a considerable task.

For the purpose of organising the monastic day, the year was split into two parts, because of the relatively short period of daylight during the winter months; it is interesting to note that the monks moved into the new abbey on the eve of All Saints (31 October), which marked the change from the summer to the winter timetable. On All Saints' Day (1 November) the fire

BRITISH LIBRARY

The Rule of St Benedict

would have been lit in the great warming house and kept burning night and day until Good Friday, which marked the change back to the summer timetable.

The day started for the monks at around 2am, when they were roused from sleep and descended from their dormitory to the church for the first service of the day, Vigils, which was followed by Matins and Prime. Around 9.30am they attended the daily meeting in the chapter house, to hear a reading from a chapter of the Rule of St Benedict, and to discuss business, confess faults and receive punishment. The rest of the morning would be taken up with more services in church and spiritual readings. At about mid-day they gathered in the frater (dining room) for the main meal of

The Cistercians were the first Order to use lay brothers for manual work

BRITISH LIBRARY

the day, which was followed by a short sleep in the dormitory. Several hours of manual work, reading, or copying manuscripts followed until about 5pm, when the monks went to the church for two services, None and Vespers. Afterwards they gathered in the frater for a drink, followed by a spiritual reading known as the collation which was held in the north alley of the cloister. At about 8pm they held the last service of the day, Compline, before retiring to bed.

This was a rigorous routine, only relieved by feast days and the great festivals of Christmas and Easter. A twelfth-century work of St Ailred of Rievaulx speaks of the scanty food, rough dress and toil and sweat for daily bread endured by the monk.

The choir monks did their share of manual work, but the Cistercians were the first Order to have a class of monks specifically for carrying out this

TREVOR CROUCHER

The entrance from the cloister to the church

THE BODLEIAN LIBRARY

Manuscript created at Furness Abbey

type of work – the lay brothers. Lay brothers were generally illiterate men who could not, or did not wish to, take the full profession of a choir monk, but wanted nevertheless to lead a religious life. They took simpler vows, and their service to God took the form of their devotion to manual work rather than prayer. They were housed in separate buildings within the abbey, and had their own choir in the church where they took part in simple services which they had learned by heart.

In the twelfth and thirteenth centuries this way of life proved very popular and men flocked to the abbeys. However, during the fourteenth century their numbers declined, and after the Black Death had ravaged the population, by the end of the century they seem to have ceased to exist as a separate class of monk.

Return to the cloister court and enter the south range.

SOUTH CLOISTER RANGE

The south side of the great cloister court was bounded by a large group of buildings. The Cistercians, unlike the Benedictines, insisted that the kitchen, frater (dining hall) and warming house should all be included in this one range of buildings so that the monks on kitchen duty were still near the cloister.

Warming house

The room at the east end of the south range, of which the walls still stand to a considerable height, was the monks' warming house. Originally, this was the only room where, during the winter months, a fire was allowed for the monks to warm themselves after the long cold services in the church or work in the cloister. The warming house has a single large fireplace which was inserted, together with a stone-ribbed vault, about 1190. Around the walls are various lockers and cupboards, and in the south-east corner a doorway which allowed fuel for the fire to be brought from the store outside.

Document store

The room above could only be entered from the monks' dormitory, and, like a similar room at Fountains Abbey, may have served to store the abbey's documents and charters. Its first use was as a tracing-room, where the master mason designed the tracery of the great rose window in the west front of the church, etching its design into the paving of its floor.

Refectory

West of the warming house was the frater or refectory which, unusually in a Cistercian monastery, was built

Right: The fireplace in the warming house

The refectory would have been similar to this one at Cleeve Abbey (Reconstruction by Terry Ball)

over a vaulted undercroft and lit by well-proportioned, round-headed windows, one of which survives in its east wall. The floor level of the frater was about 1.6m (5ft) above cloister level, and reached by a flight of steps. During meals, the monks ate in strict silence, while one monk read from the scriptures, standing in a pulpit built into the west wall. Although this pulpit has vanished, its position is marked by a thickening in the wall.

The meals served here were very basic, consisting mainly of vegetables and bread, washed down by beer. Despite observing silence, the monks would have used a system of hand signals to communicate with the servers, as Benedictine monks still do today.

Before entering the frater, the monks washed at a laver or trough, usually sited beside the frater door in the cloister. This is noticeably absent at Byland, although fragments of such a laver were found loose in the excavation.

On Saturdays, the monks who had kitchen and serving duties performed the mandatum or foot-washing ritual, washing the feet of their brethren in emulation of Christ washing the feet of the disciples. In the undercroft of the frater is a stone bench which may be the remains of the trough used in this ceremony; certainly there was a water supply into this room, for part of the lead piping still remains, set into the step of the eastern doorway from the cloister.

Kitchen

Occupying the rest of the south range, west of the frater, is the kitchen, which had two entrances from the cloister. The kitchen was remodelled in the late fourteenth or fifteenth century, when the number of monks was greatly reduced. At its west end can be seen the hatch through which food was passed into the lay brothers' lane and taken to their frater. The corresponding hatch to the monks' frater at the east end has disappeared.

The original fireplace would have been very large and probably sited in the centre of the room, but was later replaced with two smaller hearths placed back to back.

Turn right into the west range.

The fireplace in the east wall of the kitchen, with the ruined south transept in the background

Capitals and corbels in the west range

Floor tiles in the west cloister alley

WEST CLOISTER RANGE

Because there were so many lay brothers, and they followed a different routine from the choir monks, separate accommodation was provided for them in the large building on the west side of the cloister, as at most Cistercian monasteries. The whole of the first floor formed their dormitory. They used a stair at its north end near the church for their night services, and another on the east side during the day.

The architectural details, mainly capitals and corbels of simple scallop or leaf forms, show that it was finished around 1165, and that it was the earliest surviving building of the abbey to be completed. Cross walls divided the ground floor into four compartments: the lay brothers' day room and frater at the south end, which was served from the kitchen on the south side of the cloister, and, north of these, the outer parlour, where the monks might meet with visiting relatives. The other room was used for storage.

Between the west range and the cloister is a passage or lane which provided covered access from the bottom of the day stair leading from the lay brothers' dormitory at its south end, to the church. Its use as an assembly point for the lay brothers before they entered the church for services is highlighted by the remarkable series of thirty-five niches, used as seats by the lay brothers.

On the west side of the range were two large enclosed yards used by the cellarer. The western walls of these survive in the boundary wall beside the modern road. The large round-headed arch at the south end of the wall is all that remains of a late twelfth-century barn or storehouse. To the south-west, low mounds indicate the sites of other buildings, probably the lay brothers' infirmary and other domestic ranges.

After the lay brothers had ceased to form part of the community in the fourteenth century, the west range would have largely lost its original use. However, it was clearly put to some other use, as in the fifteenth century its west wall was reinforced by flying buttresses. It may have been used as a granary, as happened at Rievaulx.

From the outside (west side) of this range of buildings, walk south towards the museum.

Lay brothers' reredorter

The large building which projects from the south end of the west range, south of the kitchen, formed the lay brothers' reredorter. Down its centre can be seen the remains of an ashlar-lined stone channel, screened from the ground floor by walls which supported a row of latrine seats at first-floor level.

North of the reredorter lies a small court which originally had covered alleys on all four sides, like a small cloister. Later, a series of rooms was built on the west side.

Precinct

Church and cloister originally stood within a large walled precinct subdivided into outer and inner courts containing a variety of enclosed spaces and ancillary buildings. The Byland precinct – which also served to sequester the monks from the outside world – is about 50ha (120 acres) in extent, perhaps the largest in England.

The lane between the cloister and the west range with its row of 35 niche seats

Entry into the monastery was strictly controlled via outer gates in the precinct wall, little of which survives. Spanning the Oldstead road west of the church is one of the arches of the great inner gatehouse that marks the division between outer and inner courts. Though much ruined, enough remains of the gatehouse to determine its layout: it was divided by the arch into inner and outer porches, which were both originally stone-vaulted. The inner court contained such buildings as the guest house, granary, bakehouse and brewhouse, all now disappeared with little trace of their exact locations.

We are told by Abbot Philip (see page 27) that when the monks arrived at Byland it was a marshy site that had to be drained before building work could begin. Archaeological survey has shown that the monks achieved this by damming the stream that flowed through the precinct from the

Archway from twelfth-century barn

north-west and diverting it into an artificial leat on the valley side. Although the dam is now breached, the stream still flows along the leat as far as College Farm, where it now enters a covered conduit.

Originally it curved to the south to drive a water-powered corn mill near Brook House. The monks were thus simultaneously draining the site and using the water to power a mill.

Having drained the site, however, they needed to reintroduce water in a controlled manner for sanitation and drinking, and so built two more leats. These diverted the headwaters of the easterly-flowing Holbeck, above Wass, west to the abbey. Later, flash flooding may have been a problem, for a large earth and stone dam visible in the field north of the Oldstead road is inexplicable except as a flood barrier protecting the precinct.

Plan of the monastic precinct. The water courses in pale blue existed during the active life of the abbey, but are now dry. The darker blue indicates courses, both natural and diverted, still in existence

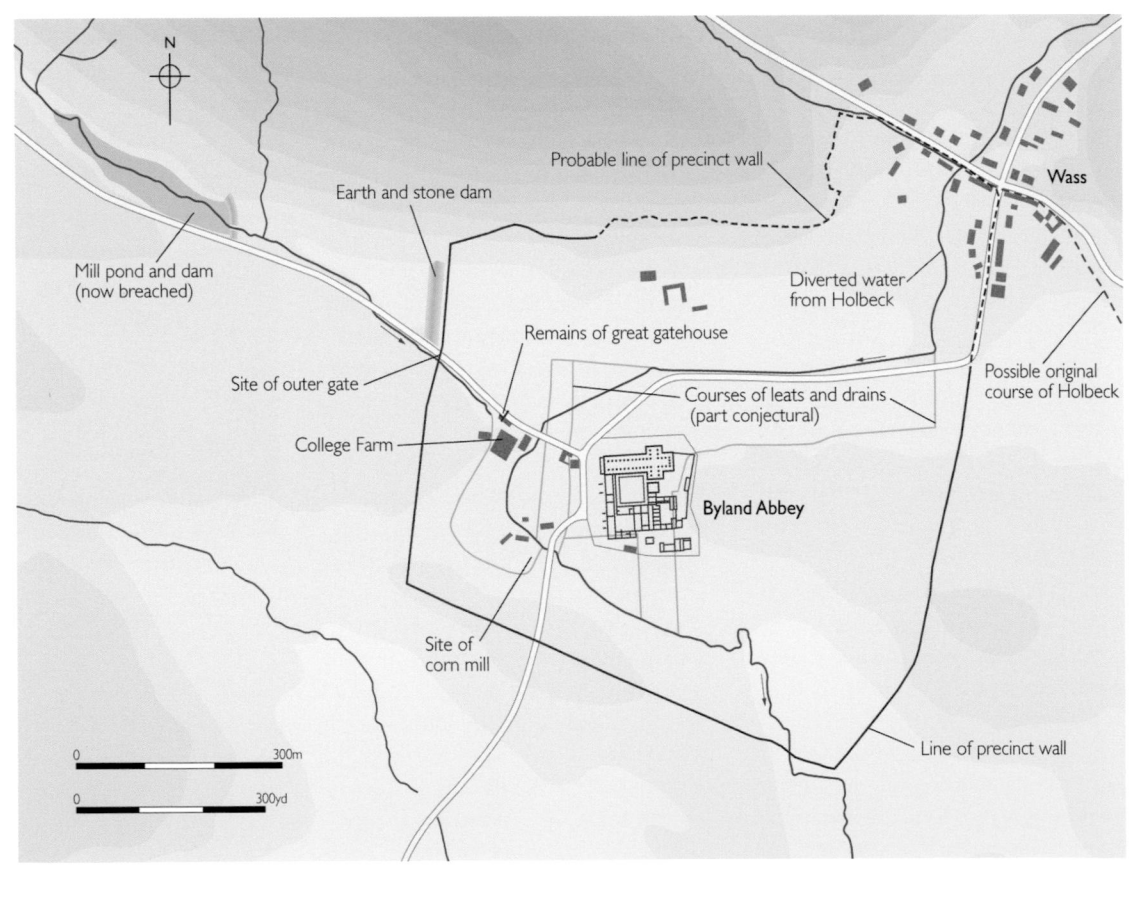

HISTORY OF THE ABBEY

❖

SAVIGNIAC BEGINNINGS

Byland Abbey began its existence as a community of the order of Savigny, one of the monastic orders which grew up in the early twelfth century with the aim of returning to a strict observance of the Rule of St Benedict. The system which St Benedict of Nursia had formulated in the sixth century for regulating his monastery at Monte Cassino was so successful that it had become one of the main forms of monastic observance throughout western Europe. It was interpreted differently at some monasteries and modified over the centuries, until by the twelfth century there were several distinctly different types of monastic order which all took St Benedict's Rule as their basis.

The order founded at Savigny in Normandy, like the Cistercian order which also grew up in the early twelfth century, was a reforming order, aiming to return to a simple observance of the Rule and eschewing the elaborately carved and painted buildings, expensive altar plate and costly vestments of other Benedictine foundations.

Although the Cistercian order proved to have greater popular success than that of Savigny, founding many new monasteries throughout Europe, the Savigniac monks were the first to establish a colony in England. In 1124, Stephen, Count of Boulogne, gave them lands at Tulketh near Preston in Lancashire. In Stephen the monks had a powerful and wealthy patron who eventually succeeded to the throne of England. For some reason the Tulketh site proved unsuitable, so in 1128 the monks moved to Furness where the new abbey soon prospered.

St Benedict, whose Rules governed the monks' lives

Stephen, Count of Boulogne, who gave lands for the building of Furness Abbey

THE TRAVELS OF THE BYLAND MONKS

Furness Abbey

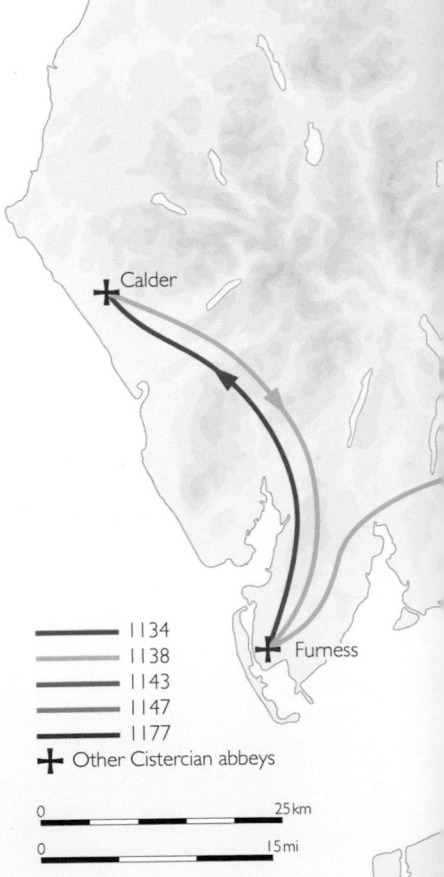

In 1134, a new colony of monks was sent, with an abbot, Gerold, to found a daughter house at Calder on the west coast of Cumberland. This was the beginning of a remarkable number of moves for the community, as each site proved unsuitable in some way. Though it was not uncommon in the Middle Ages for a newly-founded monastery to abandon its original site for a more favourable one, Byland is exceptional in that it was to be 43 years after leaving Furness and six moves later, that the monks finally established a permanent home there, in 1177. Four years after the move to Calder, the Scots invaded Cumberland and the monks gathered their possessions and fled back to Furness. However, as Gerold was unwilling to give up his rank of Abbot, they were refused entry into the mother house. Turned away from Furness, they decided to seek the help of Archbishop Thurstan at York, well known as a patron of monasticism, and set out across the Pennines.

On their way, the monks were advised by the steward of Gundreda de Albini to seek her help at Thirsk. She received them kindly, and with the agreement of her son, Roger de Mowbray, sent them to Hood, just east of Thirsk, where her relation Robert de Alneto, a former Benedictine monk of Whitby, was living as a hermit. For a short while the community joined Robert and settled at Hood. While they were there, the abbot of Furness revived the dispute begun at the gate of Furness and claimed jurisdiction over them; but abbot Gerold was not easily defeated, and in 1142 travelled to the General Chapter of abbots at Savigny and there

Rievaulx Abbey

Calder

———— 1134
———— 1138
———— 1143
———— 1147
———— 1177
✝ Other Cistercian abbeys

Furness

0   25 km
0   15 mi

won freedom from Furness. On the long return journey, Gerold fell ill: he died at York, but was buried at Hood.

Gerold was succeeded by Roger, who had been sub-cellarer at Calder, and who was to hold the office of abbot for fifty-four years, finally retiring in 1196 because of old age.

In 1143 the community moved again, this time to a site in the vill of Byland better suited to their growing numbers; but they were not to stay there for long. Byland was in Ryedale, and bordered on lands given by Walter Espec in 1131 to found the Cistercian abbey of Rievaulx. Although the site itself was adequate, it soon proved to be too close to Rievaulx: each abbey could hear the other's bells at all times of

Site changes made by the Byland monks between the foundation of their abbey in 1134 and their final settlement at Byland in 1177

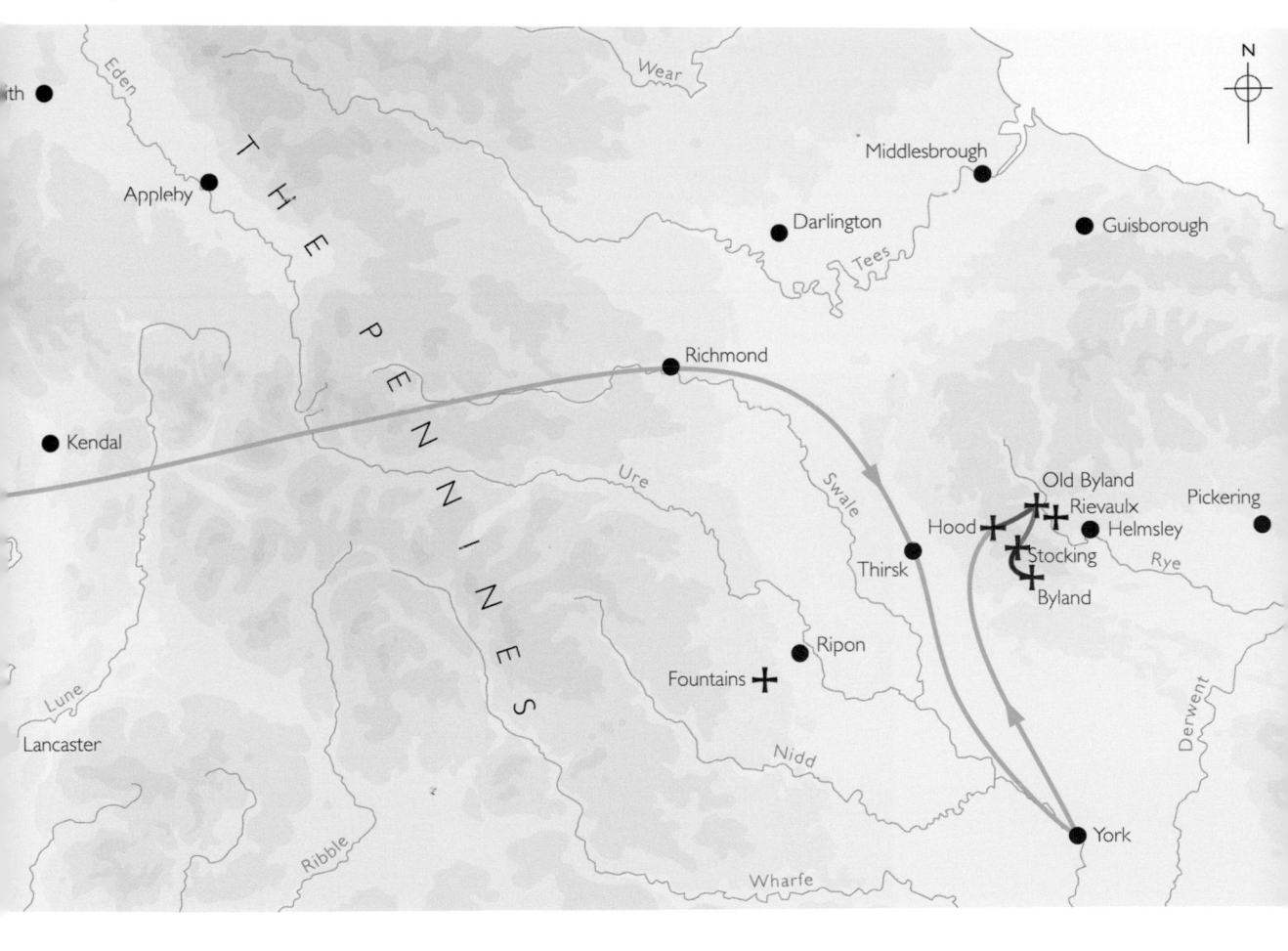

day and night, 'which was not fitting and could by no means be endured'.

As the later arrivals, it was the Savigniac monks who gave way, and in 1147 they moved south-west to a new site across the moor at Stocking – 'two carucates of waste land in the territory of Cukwald below the hill of Blakhow' – given to them by Roger de Mowbray. Here they built a small stone church with a cloister, and settled down for a while.

In the same year, the abbot of Savigny met Bernard, abbot of the Cistercian abbey of Clairvaux in Burgundy, and the prime mover behind the expansion of the Cistercian movement, and offered up his Order. Bernard accepted, and the whole Savigniac Order was merged with the Cistercian. The Byland monks must have had to change their grey habits for the Cistercian white and adopt the routines and services of Citeaux, already familiar to them from their days as neighbours of the Cistercians at Rievaulx.

In the late twelfth century, Byland was described by William of Newburgh, as one of the three shining lights of northern monasticism, beside Rievaulx and Fountains. Its

Aelred of Rievaulx as a young man: a much loved and influential personality in the Cistercian movement

Bernard of Clairvaux, the prime mover behind the development of the Cistercian Order

prestige may have been one reason why, in 1150, the abbots of Furness and the refounded Calder both revived the claim to jurisdiction over Byland. This bitter dispute dragged on until 1155, when a convocation of Cistercian abbots, headed by Aelred of Rievaulx, found in Byland's favour and placed it directly under the protection of Savigny. As an additional safeguard, Abbot Roger placed his abbey under the protection of the Archbishop of York, having all his charters and rights confirmed at the same time. Roger seems to have been a great friend of Aelred, and when the latter lay dying at Rievaulx in 1167, he anointed his body with holy oil.

The final move

Whilst at Stocking the monks acquired the site at Byland, which was waste and marshy. Thinking that it would make a better site, they soon set about clearing it.

'They began manfully to root out the woods, and by long and wide ditches to draw off the abundance of water from the marshes; and when dry land appeared they prepared for themselves an ample, fitting and worthy site in the eastern part of that land, between Whiteker and the foot of the hill of Cambe, that is next to Burtoft and Bersclyve, where they built their fair and great Church, as it now appears. May the All Highest perfect and preserve it for evermore. And so they removed thither from Stockyng on the eve of All Saints, in the year of our Lord's incarnation, 1177 and there, God willing, they shall prosperously remain forever.'

So wrote Abbot Philip in 1197 when he set down the history of the house, related to him by Abbot Roger and other members of the monastery.

THE FOUNDING OF BYLAND

The earliest surviving building on the site is the west range, which provided accommodation for the lay brothers. Completed by about 1165, it may indicate that the lay brothers had occupied the site in advance of the choir monks, to help with the construction of the buildings.

View northwards down the west cloister range, which provided accommodation for the lay brothers

This plan shows the building phases of the upper parts of the church, which was built between 1175 and 1195. It is taken at the level of the aisle windows and shows the vaulting pattern above the aisles and the stairs to the dormitories at first-floor level in the east and west ranges. The building sequence can be worked out with some certainty from the existing ruins and stones recovered during excavation

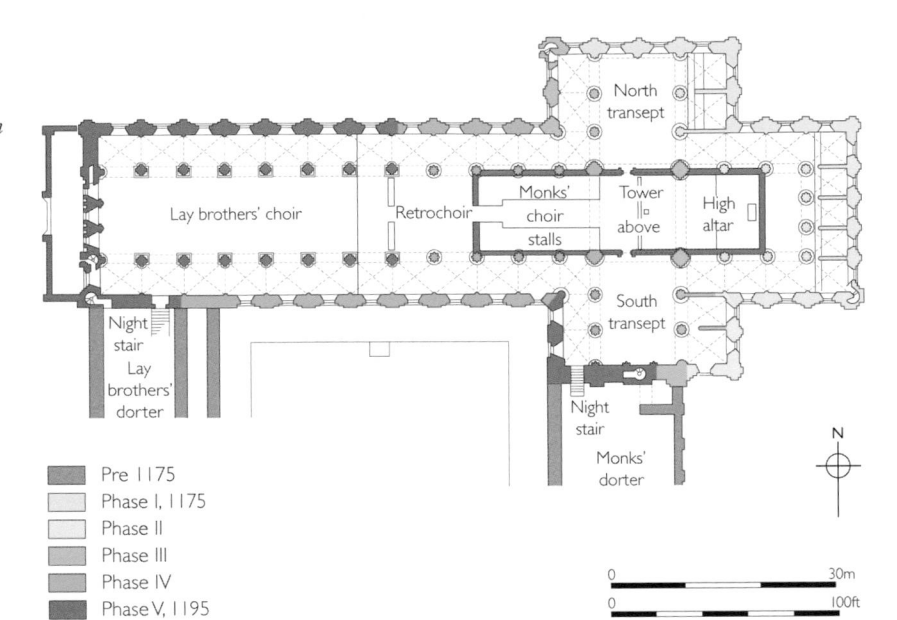

- Pre 1175
- Phase I, 1175
- Phase II
- Phase III
- Phase IV
- Phase V, 1195

0   30m
0   100ft

An angel assists in the building of an abbey, in a twelfth-century illustration from Durham Cathedral Priory

When the monks first moved here from Stocking in 1177, most of the monastic buildings were completed, but construction of the church had barely begun. We know that it was finished in the 1190s and was built around a temporary church which was progressively demolished as parts of the new church became usable.

When first built, this new church was the largest Cistercian church in Britain, and a building of such scale indicates a large community. Although we have no figures for the twelfth century, when the monastery was at its peak, in 1231 it was stipulated that the number of choir monks should not exceed eighty, and that no more lay brothers be recruited until their numbers had fallen below one hundred and sixty.

As at most abbeys, the later years of Byland saw a reduction in the number of monks, with a small number using buildings that had been designed for hundreds. This led to considerable changes in the way the buildings were used, and constant alterations were underway to convert buildings to new uses, reducing some and enlarging others.

❖ THE MONASTIC ECONOMY ❖

Agricultural labour was not only an essential tenet of Cistercian monastic life, but also an economic necessity, as monasteries were at first forbidden the traditional sources of revenue such as tithes and rents. It was the fruits of their labours that provided the monks with a substantial income, making possible the construction of the extensive buildings of the monastery.

BIBLIOTHEQUE MUNICIPALE, DIJON

Reaping monk, from an illuminated manuscript

The Cistercians were great agriculturalists, and in the twelfth century developed a system of running their estates from outlying farms known as granges, which were mainly devoted to the rearing of sheep. Their flocks numbered many thousands. The annual wool clip of Byland was gathered and sorted in the woolhouse at nearby Thorpe, before being packed and exported abroad. During abbot Roger's tenure the abbey grew immensely wealthy, acquiring large local landholdings and the revenues from several churches, as well as land as far afield

as Warcop and Asby in Cumbria, mines in the West Riding of Yorkshire, freedom from many local and national taxes and tolls, and free passage for its goods through the ports.

The labour force necessary to administer the economy of the abbeys was created – the lay brothers (see page 17).

Byland seems to have suffered particularly badly during the years of plague, and by 1381 there were only eleven monks and three lay brothers. Thereafter the Cistercians turned their estates over to a system of servants and tenancies, and as a result moved closer to a more worldly lifestyle.

TRINITY COLLEGE, CAMBRIDGE

Page from agricultural treatise written at Byland

Right: A medieval depiction of shepherds with sheep

BRITISH LIBRARY

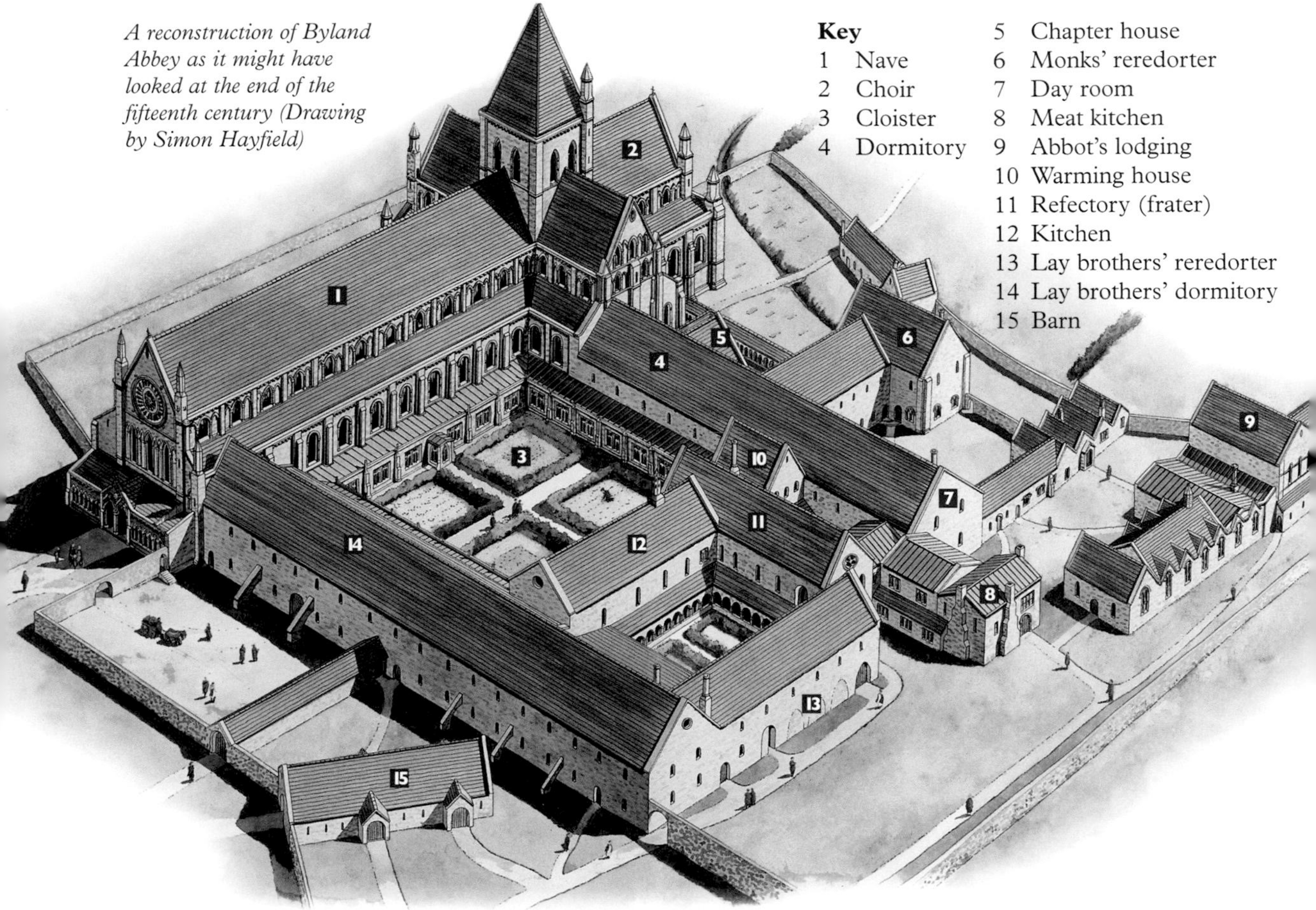

A reconstruction of Byland Abbey as it might have looked at the end of the fifteenth century (Drawing by Simon Hayfield)

Key

1 Nave
2 Choir
3 Cloister
4 Dormitory
5 Chapter house
6 Monks' reredorter
7 Day room
8 Meat kitchen
9 Abbot's lodging
10 Warming house
11 Refectory (frater)
12 Kitchen
13 Lay brothers' reredorter
14 Lay brothers' dormitory
15 Barn

PUBLIC RECORD OFFICE

THE DISSOLUTION OF THE MONASTERIES

The routine of monastic life continued relatively uninterrupted at Byland until the great changes of Henry VIII's reign. These were to see the end of all the monasteries in Britain.

Byland's one mention in national events occurred in 1322, when the army of King Edward II was surprised and defeated by an invading Scottish force at nearby Shaws Moor, and the abbey was pillaged by the Scots.

In 1538 the abbey's annual income was £295, and besides

Abbot John Ledes there were twenty-five choir monks, who surrendered the buildings and all the abbey's property to Henry VIII's Suppression Commissioners. The monks were granted pensions of about £6 each with the abbot receiving £50. After they left, the buildings were gutted of all saleable items, including the altar plate, furnishings and timber and lead from the roofs. Stripped of their roofs, the buildings would soon have become ruinous, a process hastened no doubt by local people who took stone to build their cottages. In 1540 the King granted the site to Sir William Pickering.

LATER HISTORY

Over the subsequent centuries the Abbey buildings passed to the families of Wotton, Stapylton and Wombwell.

Nearly 400 years after its demise as a monastery, Byland was placed, in 1921, in the guardianship of the Office of Works, which cleared and preserved the ruins. It is now in the care of English Heritage.

Opposite below: Henry VIII depicted in an initial letter from the document containing the national valuation of all church property, ordered in 1535

Below: Before and after excavation of the nave early this century

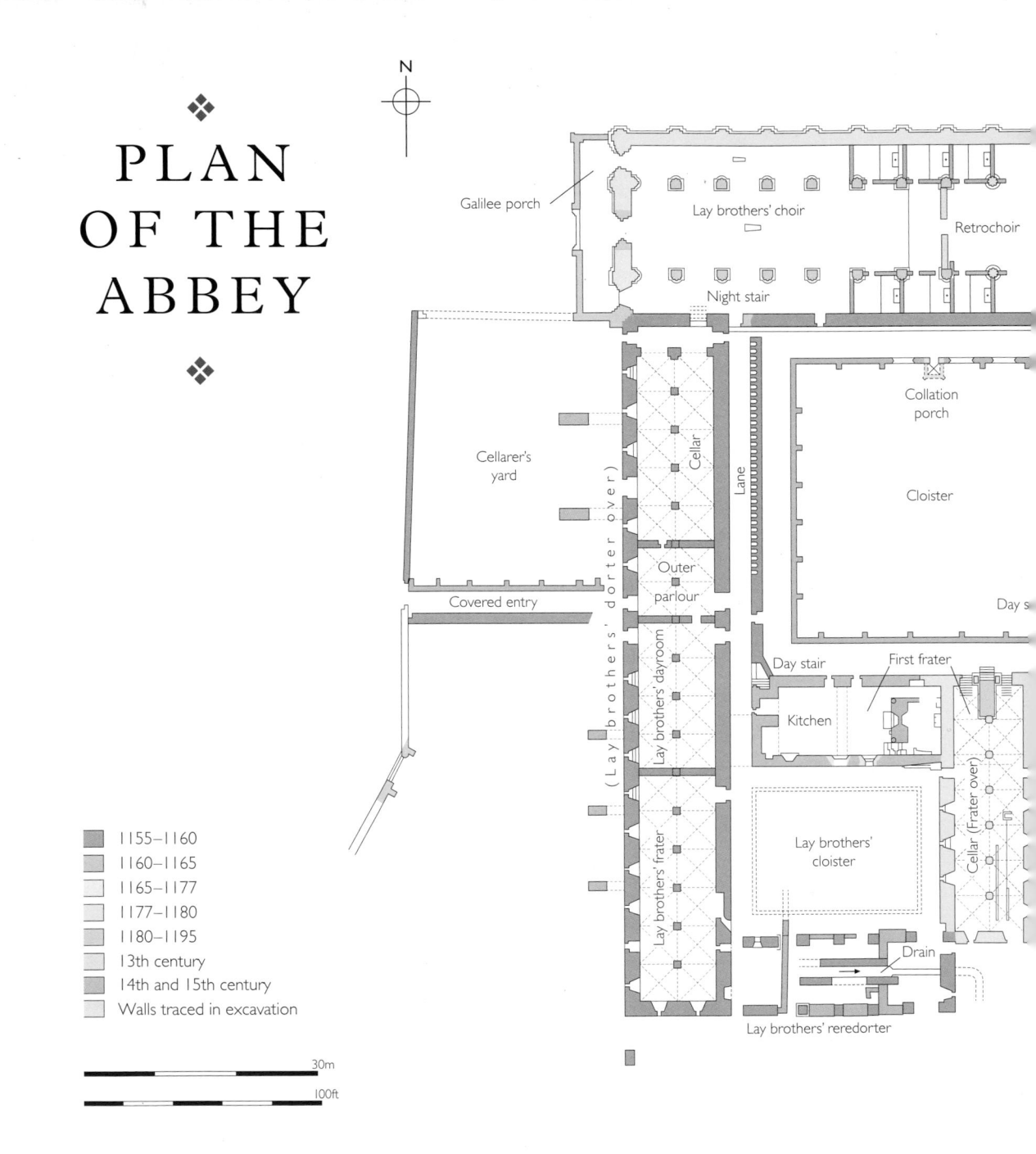

PLAN
OF THE
ABBEY

N

Galilee porch

Lay brothers' choir

Retrochoir

Night stair

Collation porch

Cellarer's yard

Cellar

Lane

Cloister

(Lay brothers' dorter over)

Covered entry

Outer parlour

Day s

Day stair

First frater

Lay brothers' dayroom

Kitchen

Cellar (Frater over)

Lay brothers' frater

Lay brothers' cloister

Drain

Lay brothers' reredorter

1155–1160
1160–1165
1165–1177
1177–1180
1180–1195
13th century
14th and 15th century
Walls traced in excavation

30m

100ft